K-2

COMMUNITY WORKERS

A Paramedic's Job

MIGUEL ROSARIO

Cavendish
Square

New York

Published in 2015 by Cavendish Square Publishing, LLC
243 5th Avenue, Suite 136, New York, NY 10016

Library of Congress Cataloging-in-Publication Data

Rosario, Miguel.
A paramedic's job / Miguel Rosario.
pages cm. — (Community workers)
Includes index.
ISBN 978-1-62712-996-1 (hardcover) ISBN 978-1-62712-997-8 (paperback) ISBN 978-1-62712-998-5 (ebook)
1. Emergency medical services—Juvenile literature. 2. Emergency medical technicians—Juvenile literature. I. Title.
RA645.5.R665 2015
362.18—dc23
2013050642

Editorial Director: Dean Miller
Editor: Amy Hayes
Copy Editor: Wendy Reynolds
Art Director: Jeffrey Talbot
Designer: Douglas Brooks
Photo Researcher: J8 Media
Production Manager: Jennifer Ryder-Talbot
Production Editor: David McNamara

The photographs in this book are used by permission and through the courtesy of: Cover photo by Blend Images - Paul Burns / Brand X Pictures / Getty Images; Tyler Olson / Shutterstock.com, 5; Tyler Olson / Shutterstock.com, 7; Richard Price / The Image Bank / Getty Images, 9; Kablonk / SuperStock, 11; Tyler Olson / Shutterstock.com, 13; Tyler Olson / Shutterstock.com, 15; © IStockphoto.com / leaf, 17; © IStockphoto.com / monkeybusinessimages, 19; Kablonk! / Masterfile, 21.

Printed in the United States of America

Contents

We are **paramedics.**

Paramedics help people who
are sick or hurt.

We work in an **ambulance**.

We get a call on the radio.

A call means someone needs help.

It's an **emergency!**

Someone is sick.

We drive quickly to where the emergency is.

We are here!

We put the emergency **kit** on the **stretcher**.

We pull the stretcher out of the ambulance.

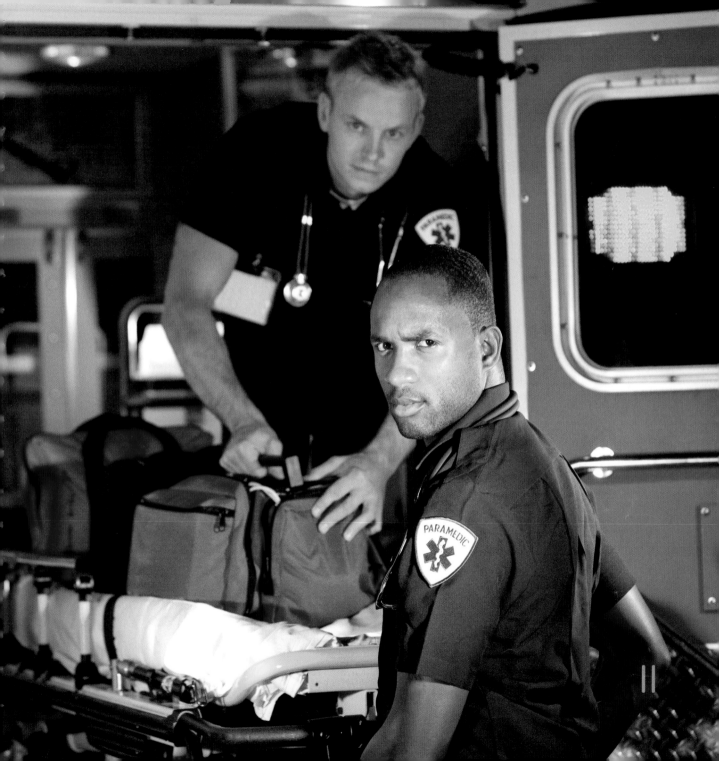

There's a woman who is sick!

We check to see if we can help.

Then we put her on the stretcher.

13

We put the woman in
the ambulance.

We will take her to the hospital.

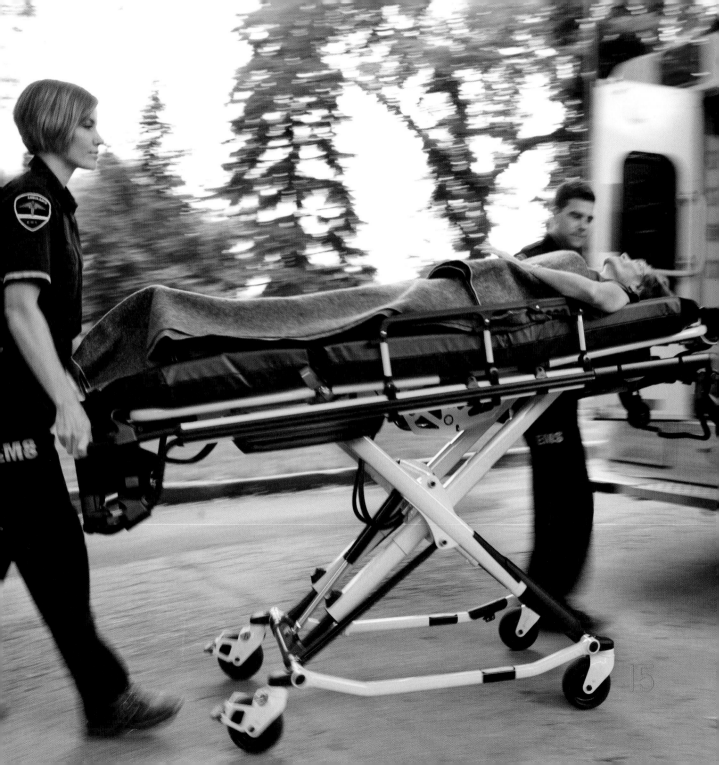

I stay in the back of
the ambulance.

I **treat** the sick person.

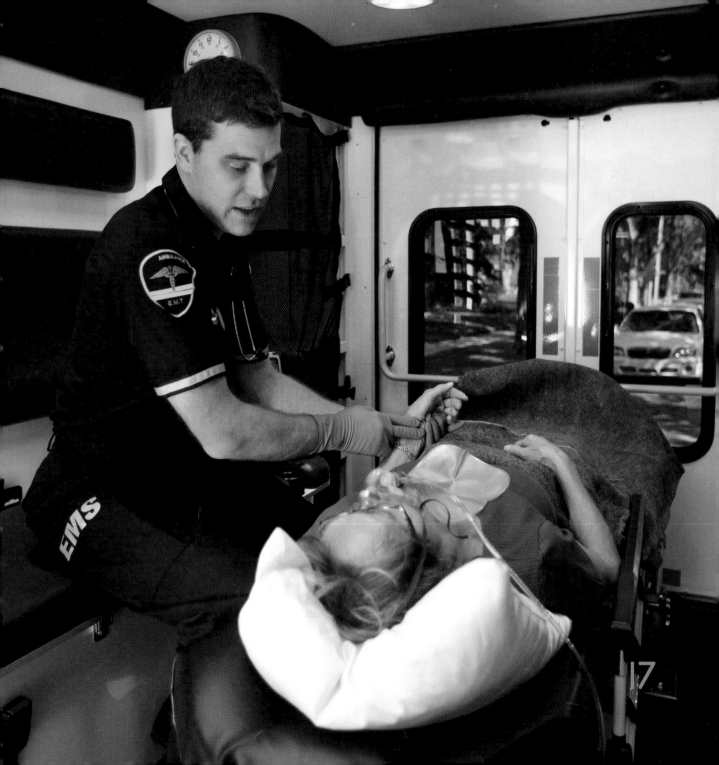

We are at the hospital.

A doctor meets us at the door.

We tell the doctor what is wrong with the **patient**.

Our job is done.

Now we are ready for our next emergency.

21

Words to Know

ambulance (**am**-byu-lents) a vehicle that is used to take someone to the hospital

emergency (ee-**mir**-jent-see) a problem that needs attention right away

kit (**kit**) a bag of supplies used to treat someone

paramedics (pa-rah-**me**-diks) workers who treat people during an emergency

patient (**pey**-shent) a person who the doctor or paramedic treats

stretcher (**stre**-cher) a cot with wheels to move someone who is hurt or sick

treat (**treet**) to care for someone who is sick or hurt

Find Out More

Books

Ambulances
by Marcia S. Freeman, Capstone Press

Emergency!
by Gail Gibbons, Holiday House

Impatient Pamela Says Learn How to Call 9-1-1
by Mary Koski and Lori Collins, Trellis Publishing

Website

TriStar Centennial Medical Center
tristarcentennial.com/your-health/kidshealth/index. dot?id=82172&mainCategory=3

Index